Worship Spaces: Teach With Them

Michael G. Bausch

About the cover: The cover image is from the sanctuary of the St. John's United Church of Christ, Hartford, Wisconsin. These windows are absolutely gorgeous in any kind of light. The church has recently closed so the windows are, sadly, no longer available for public view.

ISBN 9798367952001

Table of Contents

Introduction

St. John's United Church of Christ, Hartford, Wisconsin

The architecture of sacred spaces invites congregations to remember their connection to the stories and symbols of the faith of the congregations while reminding them of their central mission in the world

Worship leaders often presume people know the "language" of their worship spaces. What an opportunity it is to be able to help people look at what's right in front of them – and to see it fresh and new! The windows are telling stories, as is the altar or communion table. The position of the pulpit tells a story; the light fixtures just might contain hidden messages; and certainly where you have or have not placed the baptismal fount says something about the congregation's relationship with the sacrament.

Much may be gained from preaching architecture. It can:

- Capture the attention of those in the congregation who are curious, who have an interest and aptitude for buildings and architecture, and who have a personal investment in the building and upkeep of the space.
- Provide a valuable multisensory learning experience as the congregation focuses their visual attention on common elements of the church while listening to the preacher's observations and insights.
- Acknowledge those who have sat through worship services and focused their attention on some of the visual details in the sanctuary while listening to sermons, music, and prayers.
- Affirm the long history of a congregation as you speak of the origins of its church and the history of the building(s).
- Recall and affirm the positive memories long-term members have for their church.
- Develop a sense of unity and boost a sense of congregational identity as the congregation's relationship to the space is named and nurtured in new ways.
- Enrich the worship experience for those eager to learn more about the church they've chosen for worship.
- Heighten awareness of the particulars of a sacred space and stimulate reflection on what makes a space holy.

Chapter 1

The Worship Space

" . . . tongues in trees, books in the running brooks, sermons in stones, good in everything . . . "

William Shakespeare

" . . . when your children ask in time to come, 'What do those stones mean to you?' then you shall tell them . . . so these stones shall be . . . a memorial forever."

Joshua 4:6-7

As Shakespeare poetically noted, the world around us is full of sermons waiting to be preached. Joshua told the people crossing over the Jordan River to put up a tower of stones to capture the children's attention. Seeing the stones, the children would ask why the stones were there, and the children's parents could then tell the story of the significance of that place.

Our worship spaces are similar monuments to memory, full of stories of the congregation and its reasons for being, as well as of the people who gave their time, energy, and donations to build and sustain the space.

Each sanctuary has stories to tell with mysterious symbols to describe, and, in a world where people ask few questions for fear of appearing ignorant, who better to ask those questions than a preacher?

A wonderful starting point for beginning a process of preaching architecture is to ask the children or youth what they notice in a sanctuary and to invite them to ask their questions about things the children or youth have seen. The young are curious, and, as visually oriented as they are, have noticed things that caught their attention.

A couple of children's messages inviting these questions about the sanctuary can then lead into a series of sermons about the architectural forms (layout, windows, furnishings, fabrics, symbols) and the stories behind the forms.

I've practiced this process with four congregations I have served. Each time I've received comments from people who say they have worshipped their whole lives in that sanctuary and never heard a sermon telling about the connections with the sanctuary and windows to biblical stories or have never heard anyone talk about the symbols the people have noticed on the sanctuary walls, woodwork, baptismal founts, pulpits, lecterns, and altars.

These spaces we inhabit for worship have been purposefully designed by church architects to serve the function of a worshipping community. Those who use the spaces give these enclosures different names. They might be called a "house of God" or a "temple," perhaps a "house of worship" or a "meeting house" or meeting place. The building might even be called a "church" or "chapel", a "synagogue" or "mosque."

The Sanctuary

For our purposes in this book, we'll use the term "sanctuary" to refer to a worship space.

The word "sanctuary" comes from the Latin "sanctus," or "holy." It is an enclosure of some kind that is considered a place set apart, a holy space within a part of nature or in a building. This space in nature may be bounded by a group of trees, or bushes, or stones, and in a building, by walls and a ceiling.

The term sanctuary speaks of a space that also may be subdivided into smaller, discrete spaces having additional functions within the larger space. Many sanctuaries include a narthex at the entrance to the worship space; a nave, where the congregation is seated or stands; and a chancel, where worship leaders gather around sacred furnishings such as an altar, communion table, or pulpit. Some sanctuaries also might include a smaller chapel area extending off to the sides of the nave.

Let's consider each of these spaces as found within a sanctuary.

The Narthex

The narthex, sometimes also called a foyer, is the entrance area between the front doors and the doors to the worship area or nave. The term "foyer" is French for the place of the hearth or fireplace, a focal point in a room. Some church foyers are very comfortable spaces with chairs, lamps, tables, literature racks, and a guest book. These all invite people into the "home" that is the church.

The Latin term "narthex" refers to a similar kind of area, with the additional meaning that once upon a time the area was a place to keep a smaller space separate from the nave reserved for penitents and others who were not welcomed into the nave. In a sense, it implies the entryway just outside the nave is a place of preparation for full participation in the life of the worship community.

The Nave

The nave is the central part of the worship sanctuary, where most people come to be seated, usually with an aisle or aisles separating two or more seating sections. The term comes from the Latin word for ship, which could refer to the story of Noah and the ark of salvation or to Gospel stories with Jesus and disciples in boats on Galilee.

Many sanctuaries look or feel like a ship, with the beams in the ceiling reminiscent of how one imagines a covered ship, such as Noah's ark. I've been in one sanctuary shaped like that ark that even had portholes for the entry door windows, and the porthole theme continued in each of the stained glass windows on the sides of the nave. Another sanctuary I know had blue-green colored windows to evoke the colors of the sea outside the "ark" of the church.

If a sanctuary evokes feelings of being in a boat, then some meanings we might draw would be how the humans who gather there are kept safe and nurtured for a while and then sent out again to the "dry land" of the world that lies fresh before them as they "disembark" as disciples.

While the building is of course anchored to the ground, the concept of church as a "boat" assumes a metaphorical kind of movement: The church is on the move rather than moored, and this boat navigates the waters of life while protecting its occupants from a remembered pre-creation watery chaos (see Genesis 1:1) or the deep of the abyss.

The Chancel

The chancel is the area around the altar, usually reserved for the clergy, choir, and lay leaders of worship. The term is from a Latin word referring to lattices or crossbars, a reference to communion railings or other wooden structures separating the altar area from the nave. Sometimes there are steps leading up, denoting going upward, and toward the sky/heaven or a sacred precinct. These steps may be a set of three to add to any trinitarian symbolism found elsewhere in a particular sanctuary.

The chancel typically contains an altar or communion table, along with a pulpit, a lectern, an organ/piano, and seating for clergy and the choir.

Spending Time With Your Worship Space

A worship leader wanting to preach the architecture of a holy space needs to spend time in that space to simply look around and pay attention to what is seen. Bring a notebook and pen or a recording device to record observations and maybe a camera to take pictures of what you notice.

A way to structure your experience might be to follow a "form-content-meaning" kind of process. Art historians sometimes use the terms "icon-iconography-iconology" to refer to a similar way to begin to analyze a work of art or architecture. The icon is the work of art itself, iconography is all that's written about that work, and iconology includes the meanings drawn from it all.

"There is evidence that congregations, even auditory ones, enjoy the pairing of sound with sight when it is done tastefully, sparingly, gracefully, and gradually."

Michael Bausch

Using this "form-content-meaning" method is a helpful way to begin to access all that is present in a worship space. Essentially the viewer identifies three things:

The *form* of the thing you looking at. Simply identify the kind of art or architecture it is (for example, painting, photography, fabric, sanctuary architecture) and the materials used to construct it. You are answering a basic question, "What is it? What is this thing?"

The *content* of the thing. What do you see? Look at it, and notice all the details of the work, such as colors, shapes, figures, and what you understand to be the story being told. The basic question you're asking is, "What's the story? What's going on, and why?"

The *meaning* of the thing and its story. This is where we start drawing out what the form and its content mean: what the form meant originally in the Christian story, what the form meant to those who included it in the sanctuary, what the form might have meant for those who worshipped here in the past, and what the form might mean for us now and down the road. What is the thing, the form, trying to tell you – and why? What does it have to do with God and the life, work, ministry, and mission of the church?

It is important that a preacher use all three aspects of this "form-content-meaning" process while experiencing the architecture, contents, and fabrics of the worship space. Sometimes the meanings are what come later, after further thought and the movement of the Spirit, and it is worth the wait.

To preach architecture, furnishings, and fabrics requires more than a simple description of what they are, because the listeners will want to connect with the stories that are told (the content of what you're looking at) and will welcome the meanings you draw as you move the listeners forward along their missional path as a worship community.

A Self-Guided Tour of A Worship Space

You might start by wandering the entire area of the sanctuary, starting from the main entrance, next into the foyer or narthex, and then to the nave and chancel.

Before you enter the nave, pause for a moment to remember this is someone's sacred space. When I've taken groups to St. Peter's Basilica in Rome, I've preceded them in and turned around so I could face them as they encounter the space for the first time: It is a moment of awe for them, and I see their eyes open wide and hear audible gasps. Other less grand worship spaces may evoke less of a response, and yet each sanctuary has its own spirit and testimony.

As you enter, experience the whole space for a while as you see it with fresh eyes. Take the time you need with this new introduction to your worship space and pay attention to your initial reactions with feelings and thoughts.

Consider what's there: the whole, and then the parts: the structure, shape, colors, smells, textures, flooring, windows, walls, ceiling, ornamentation, symbols, furnishings. As you're drawn into the space, notice the various "forms" of the things you see: What questions do they inspire, and what stories do they hold? What meanings might you draw from what you see?

After a few moments of this, remember you might be "preaching" your experience and what you see here, so make notes on themes and approaches you might use in any future sermon series.

After a walk-through from the entryway to the narthex and into the nave and chancel, you might choose to do any of the following. While this is a numbered list, you may certainly pick and choose these "exercises."

1. Sit where you usually sit and relax in place. Breathe, pray, meditate, and center yourself in that space. Begin to notice what you feel: your feet on the floor, the soft or hard surface of the seat, your back against the pew or chair.
2. Let your mind consider the history of the space, the years it's been used, the people who've been important to it. Think about the occasions that have brought people in: weekly worship, weddings, baptisms, funerals.
3. What energy is in the space, and how does it smell? Be aware of how all your senses are attuned to your experience there.
4. Look around. What do you see? Make a list of the items in the space and the questions you have about how the items fit into worship. What furnishings do you see? Ask yourself why these things are there?
5. What do you notice about the general order of the sanctuary: Is it clean, with everything in its proper place, or is it cluttered and full of things that don't seem to relate to each other in a meaningful way?
6. Look up to the ceiling. As you look at the structure of the ceiling, you might simply count the beams. Some churches will have three, evoking the trinity, but more likely six, evoking the six days of creation, while the whole structure itself makes the seventh, the day of rest and worship.
    a. Some churches have one kind of ceiling in the nave and a different ceiling for the chancel, or the area directly above the communion table, altar, pulpit, and lectern. While a beamed ceiling may rise above the nave, the ceiling above the chancel area may be plaster panels angled at each other, or even scalloped, to evoke a sense of sky or clouds while adding to the acoustical quality of the space.
    b. Sometimes the chancel area is enclosed in a large arch, as if to call forth the image of a shrine containing the "holy of holies," which might be the altar, the Bible, the communion table, and/or other furnishings that evoke the sense of that space set aside for the clergy, perhaps the choir, sometimes the organ and organ pipes, and usually a cross.

7. Notice the ceiling light fixtures. How many chandeliers are there, if any? One church I served had ten, with five on each side, evoking the Ten Commandments and the light they shed upon a community of faith. When I pointed this out in a sermon in that church, the custodian told me there were four light fixtures in each one, making 40 lights. It seemed this further hinted at the Noah story, with the ark-like sanctuary and the blue-green sea windows, and the lights representing the 40 days and 40 nights. Without knowing if this were the original architectural intent, it did provide an interesting connection. Other sanctuaries have groups of six or seven fixtures, all playing off 6-7-8-12 symbolisms with the numbers (see No. 12 below for meanings of the numbers).

8. How many candles are in the sanctuary and where are they located? Why is this, do you think? Are they electric, wax, or paraffin? What are these – and their placement – saying about worship, liturgy, and light source?

9. Determine the orientation of the sanctuary. What direction does it face (north, south, east, or west)? What significance, if any, is this direction? Synagogues, for example, face Jerusalem. Some churches follow that convention. Still others are more functionally situated to take advantage of the morning or evening light with a south-north orientation.

10. What are the windows like? Are they clear, or are they colored? Do they contain stories, symbols, or color alone? Why, and what significance do they bring to the worship space? See the next chapter for more discussion on windows, colors, and stories.

11. Where does music come from? Where are any bells, chimes, organ pipes, pianos, guitars, drums, and sound systems located? How do these fit into the design of the sanctuary? Is there projection equipment such as a screen and projector, and how do these fit into the worship architecture? Are there any religious symbols connected to these items? For example, sometimes a central cross is affixed to the center front of organ pipes if they are located at the front wall of the chancel area.

12. Pay attention to groupings of similar things such as windowpanes, archways, or carvings in wooden backdrops or furnishings. Notice numbers of things: groupings of three might represent the Trinity, five might point to the Pentateuch or the first five books of Moses, six might represent the six days of the week,

seven might represent the fullness of six days of creation and one day of rest, eight might represent a fresh beginning (the day after the seventh day) or that which transcends both earthly reality (the number 6) and heavenly reality (the number 7), and 12 might represent the 12 disciples.

13. What symbols do you notice, such as Greek or Latin symbols or words on wooden or painted surfaces or fabrics? Common symbols are the Greek letters alpha and omega (the first and last letters of the Greek alphabet, representing beginning and end) and the chi and rho (the X and P, or the first two letters of the name "Christ" in Greek). You might also notice a cross with the Latin INRI, for Iesus Nazorenus Rex Iudaeorum, "Jesus the Nazarene, King of the Jews," as the Roman inscription ordered placed on the cross. One entire sermon could be devoted to these Greek and Latin symbols and their origins and stories.

14. A central symbol in Christianity is a cross. Is there a central cross and where is that located? What does the location seem to say about Christian faith, this particular worship sanctuary, and the gathered community? Is there an implied cross in the very shape of this sanctuary? Is the central aisle a long one leading to the chancel (evoking a Latin cross), or is it about the same length as the width of the sanctuary (a Greek cross)?

a. How many walls do you see? Sometimes what appear to be four walls is actually a structure with eight, representing the fresh beginning of the eighth day, the first day of the new creation, or the day after the Resurrection. Where is the center of the room, and what does that say about the architecture and the congregation that gathers there? Is the center of the room where the congregation sits, and what does that say about this space as "church."

15. Get up and move around, sitting in different parts of the sanctuary. Think of the people you know and where they sit, and go there to see what they see. Jot down what you notice about these different vantage points.

16. Are there memorial plaques showing names of various people over time who have given windows, bells, musical equipment, furnishings, founts, altars, hymnals, or other things found in the sanctuary? What stories are added to these features by the memories of these persons? What are some of the forgotten stories someone might be able to tell?

17. Make a note to return to the sanctuary after a worship service to pay attention to what your senses notice: Can you feel the warmth and pick up the scent of colognes and perfumes? What energy remains, if any? Consider the mystery of the gathering, what transpired, what it meant for all of you to have been there as a community of faith.

18. Come to the sanctuary at different times of the day and night to see what the different light or shadow adds or subtracts to the environment. What changes at different times?

19. Going deeper: What does the architecture reflect about the history of the congregation? Does the architecture fit the era when the church was founded? How does the architecture reflect the central Christian theological themes common to most churches? What interests and life stories of the founders are found in the sanctuary? How well do the structure and space fit the perceived mission of the church, and what do the structure and space say about the approach of the church to worship and preaching? Having old photographs of the space will help you grasp some of the history and passage of time.

Shapes in Church Architecture

Worship spaces come in different shapes. One shape might be a circle, representing the sphere of earth and the dome of heaven. This shape is found in mosques, often with a central chandelier coming down from a dome and resting just above the heads of the worshippers, representing the lights from the dome of heaven coming close to the congregation.

A shape with four equal sides is a square, which, like a circle, can represent an equality of balance and a reference to the four cardinal directions (north, south, east, and west). A space shaped as a circle, square, or octagon will have equidistant length and width, visible in a short central aisle. This may represent the equal arms of the shape of the Greek cross.

Sometimes what appears to be a square or rectangular shape has been altered with interior wall angles to become an octagon. This is very subtly done and sometimes takes a while to notice. A nave with an octagonal shape might represent a sense of equality as well as the eighth day of creation, a fresh beginning, when God and humans begin their renewed work together.

Besides noting the length of a center aisle, counting the number of interior walls in the nave and chancel might be a way to start noticing the theological shape to a worship sanctuary.

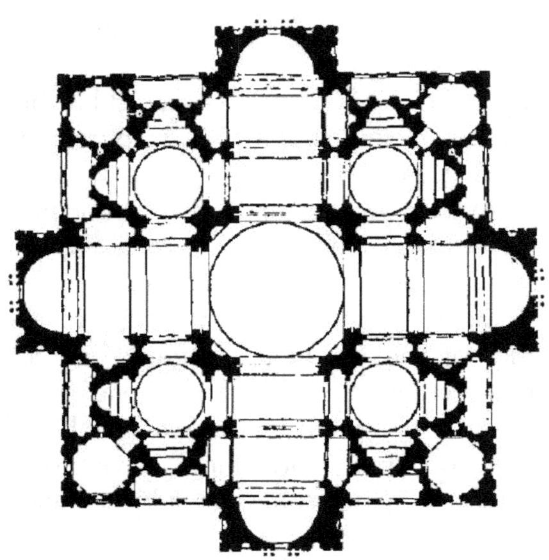

This diagram shows Bramante's Greek cross plan for St. Peter's Basilica, Rome.

A rectangular shape with four walls and a lengthy central aisle speaks more to the shape of a Latin cross. This hints at a formality and a focus on the leadership of the church, with the aisle used for ceremonial processionals and recessionals with clergy and choir.

The long rectangular sanctuary, as in a basilica such as St. Peter's in Rome, is shaped as a Latin cross, with the arms at the end of the nave where the chancel begins and the vertical of the cross extending from the entrance of the nave all the way to the front wall of the chancel. The long aisle facilitates formal processionals that end at the high altar, which is at the center of the crossing of the vertical and the horizontal arms of the cruciform shape. The high altar, where the Pope celebrates the mass, becomes the focus of the mass and the liturgy.

While these shapes may represent theological and liturgical commitments of a particular worship community, it is good to remember that the space itself is formed to follow particular functions.

Think about other public spaces such as lecture halls, concert halls, theaters-in-the-round, and amphitheaters, and then consider how your worship sanctuary compares. Notice how the form follows the function and how the space fits the human relationship of presenters and audience and the kind of engagement that will be invited. Will the audience become a part of the performance? Will the audience be expected to simply sit and listen? Will the audience need to hear well and see well? Is there a priority given to speaking and listening or to watching and seeing or both?

Where is the architectural center of the space, and what does that say about the purpose of the gathering and the design of what happens in that space? Is there a difference between the actual center of the space and the perceived center? That is, is the chancel the central focus and center of the space and event rather than the actual center somewhere in the audience?

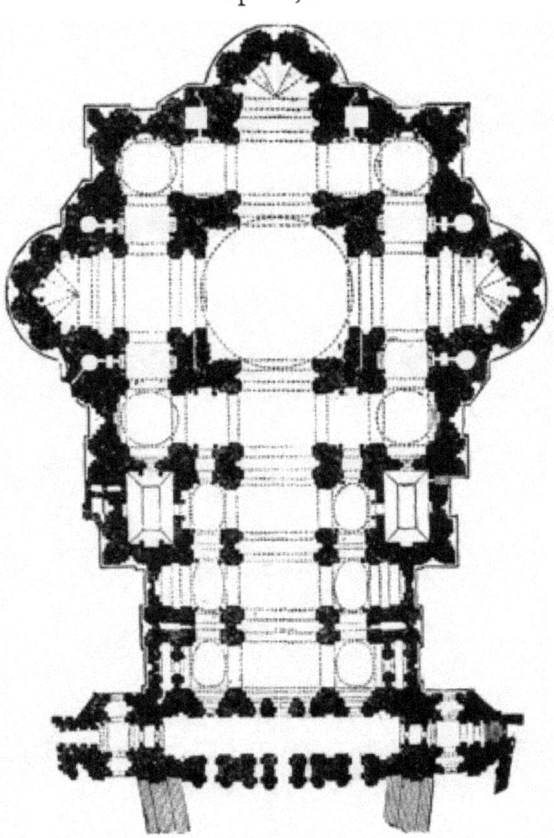

This diagram shows Rafael's Latin cross design for St. Peter's Basilica, Rome.

In a worship space, what do the locations of these centers say about God, the community, Jesus Christ, worship, whom we are, whom we're called to be, where we're called to go?

In the next chapter, we'll take an in-depth look at the chancel, furnishings, and fabrics of a worship space.

Note

Both images of the cross plans for St. Peter's Basilica are in the public domain.

Chapter 2

Chancel, Furnishings, and Fabrics

The Chancel

The chancel, as noted earlier, is the area to the front of the nave where the altar and/or communion table are located. In some churches the chancel is on a raised platform one or more steps up from the nave. Sometimes the pulpit and lectern are on the first level of the platform, with the altar/table another step or two above and behind. There may be a railing that separates pulpit/lectern from the altar/table, which makes that area by definition the chancel.

There are variations, of course, where some churches will position the communion table on the floor in front of the chancel or raised platform and still have an altar positioned at the back wall of the chancel. Where these furnishings are located is sometimes a mystery, depending on a congregation's customs, tastes, and personal decisions of various leaders.

Thinking about the difference between an altar and a communion table is important: The former is a place of sacrifice (from two Latin words "to make holy") where candles, a cross, and sometimes offering plates might be found. The communion table is where the eucharist is celebrated, where bread and wine are consecrated and shared. Sometimes there is only one altar/communion table with both functions served on the same piece of furniture.

The baptismal font is often placed in relationship to altar and table and is then a part of the chancel. In some churches the font is placed at the front entrance to the sanctuary, representing initiation into the church. In other churches, the font is located on the floor level below the platform/chancel to represent how the sacrament is a part of the community of faith, the gathered congregation. When the font is in the chancel, the font is connected to both word and sacrament, situated in relationship to pulpit, table, and altar.

Calling attention to the locations of these furnishings, their forms, and their functions – and their physical and theological relationships with each other – can be a sermon in itself.

Is there a central pulpit that serves as both the place where scripture is read and the word preached? Are there a lectern where the scripture is read and the liturgy led and a separate pulpit where the word is preached? On which side of the chancel is each located, and what does this say about that church's theology and worship? If there is a central pulpit and no lectern, might it indicate there is a unified and centralized provision of the word and its interpretation?

When there are a separate lectern and pulpit, there is a symbolic distance between both, and this might represent an interpretive freedom afforded the preacher: a space between from which the word is read and the word is preached. One might understand an invisible tension between the two with an implied difference between the Word of God (scripture) and the word of the preacher-interpreter.

There is also an interesting energy that extends from that space between pulpit and lectern out to the nave where the congregation sits, showing a relationship between scripture, preacher, and congregation together engaged in worship, liturgy, and preaching.

When preaching architecture, one might reflect on these energies as noticed in the furnishings, their function in worship, and their location in the chancel and, sometimes, the nave.

The Raised Platform

Shortly after the U.S. Civil War and into the early 1900s many of today's mainline churches (Presbyterian, Baptist, Methodist, and Congregational) used a Greek amphitheater style of architecture to bring the audience closer to the chancel and stage (platform) so the audience could better attend to the central event: preaching. Brought closer to the stage as with the ancient Greek theaters, people could better hear the preacher and choirs with a minimum of visual obstruction.

These protestant churches were beginning to also emphasize lay involvement in the life of the churches and were forming committees, structuring educational ministries, and building worship spaces that could gather this family of faith closer together in their common service.

Architectural books focusing on church construction in the 1880s sought ways to focus attention to the minister and the message while also offering the best sight lines, acoustics, and comfort for the congregation. Churches began to take on the look of classical concert and opera halls as music and preaching became central to worship life, and a kind of high urban culture of concert hall and church came together in urban areas such as New York City and Chicago and some rural areas as well.

A raised platform with three steps not only invoked the holy trinity and the elevation of holy presence but provided better acoustics in those days before microphones and amplifiers. At the same time, this helped meet the seeing and hearing needs of a congregation eager for worship, entertainment, and engagement.

Better acoustics and a sense of togetherness were accomplished with a wide platform and seating angled toward it. This also showed that worship is public and not just a private matter: Worship is best done together with other Christians. The space also provided a sense of awe and freedom with the upward reach of the ceiling and the ornamentation on the furnishings (even the clergy chairs had high backs with spires pointing upwards).

A Cruciform Shape of Nave and Chancel

As the Greek amphitheater became an architectural model for some of these free churches, they also adopted a floor plan closer to the pattern of a Greek cross, with its four equal arms. This pattern affirmed Greek themes that were matching up with the developing United States of the 19th century with its rhetoric of democracy and freedom as well as a new humanism of an equality before God. Theologically, the Greek cross with its balance, grace, and harmony could represent a common humanity before God and lift up the strength and contribution of the common man and woman gathering in the worship space.

In that shape we might see a symbolic image of God's power distributed among the people and shared with all rather than being concentrated in the hands of a few. While the clergy are leaders, there are delegation of authority and responsibility to the congregation.

Of course, not all churches were designed in the pattern of the Greek cross, as others, still having a platform and chancel, used the more elongated aisle forming a Latin cross. For these Protestant churches with a long central aisle, and those Catholic churches with a populist streak to them, the cruciform themes are still a part of the life of the church.

While the long aisle could serve grand processionals and highlight the grandeur and authority of the church, the Latin cross also is a reminder of the very nature of the cross: It was the Roman imperial instrument of torture and death for non-Roman rebels and seditionists, and it was upon such a cross (not a "Greek cross") that Jesus of Nazareth was crucified.

It is said we are to live a cruciform life. Jesus told us to take up our cross and to lose our lives for the sake of the gospel. To take up the Latin cross and remember the execution of Jesus by the powers and principalities of his day, we are called to remember all those who suffer and die for justice, righteousness, and peace in the world today.

To take up the Greek cross of equality and the heart of compassionate love is to lose our individualism and give it up for the sake of the community, to build a strong group, a strong church, a strong community.

" . . . we believe . . . the design of the environment is a choreography of the familiar and the surprising, in which the familiar has a central role, and a major function of the surprising is to render the familiar afresh."

Kent C. Bloomer and Charles W. Moore

The cross, Greek or Latin, is more than a symbol: The cross represents a form of thinking and living into which the church is called.

The church invited this theological theme into its life not only in the preached word but in the architecture of the space in which that word was preaching.

A Screen in the Chancel

The screen becomes a form through and upon which a community of faith conveys the content of the rich religious and theological imagination of the community. Part of the form, content, and meaning of the screen is its placement in the sanctuary – and the theological relationship of the screen to architectural elements already in place.

Where is the screen to be put in the sanctuary? Mostly, churches of traditional architecture find a place in the chancel area that is conducive to the temporary or permanent location of a screen. This might simply be a blank wall that serves as the screen surface, a portable screen that rests on a tripod or "legs" and is brought out for occasional use, a swath of fabric or cloth hanging above the altar, a framed screen that is permanently attached to a wall, or a motorized retractable screen that descends from a wall, a wooden beam, or metal armature.

The screen, in whatever form it takes, is always in relationship to what is already there, and that is generally a cross, an altar or communion table, and a pulpit.

The placement of a screen in relationship to cross and altar may be architecturally and theologically understood in this way:

• The altar or communion table is anchored upon the floor and the earth below, representing God's holy ground, God's protecting grace, and a community's thanksgiving to God.

• The cross is ever in relationship with the earth into which the cross is set and the heaven towards which the cross extends, and represents courage, suffering, strength, and love through the death, resurrection, and life-giving witness of Jesus the Christ. The cross symbolizes the church being called to a life of discipleship.

• The screen in relationship to cross and altar becomes the place of liminality, a doorway, a window, helping the community to imagine and live out its essential relationship to the divine story. Whereas the altar, communion table, and cross are fixed in appearance (although fabric draping, floral displays, and other temporary items may occasionally adorn the table and cross), what happens on the screen will vary. It becomes the place for showing words of prayers, scripture lessons, and hymn lyrics and for showing colors, shapes, symbols, pictures, and moving pictures. The screen shows stories freshly told and opens new ways for experiencing sermons, meditation, prayer, and instruction.

In some instances the screen might descend from above the pulpit. In this case, the screen becomes a part of the architecture of proclamation and is directly linked to the preaching and teaching function of the pastor. What is projected on the screen is understood to be part of the preached Word of God. The projected material supports and stimulates the interpretive imagination of both pastor and people by supplementing, illustrating, illuminating, and promoting the preached word.

Preaching the Chancel Furnishings

In addition to the altar, communion table, lectern, pulpit, and chairs, there are likely other furnishings and decorations in the chancel area and on the platform.

These might include:

Candles: note the number for any symbolic meaning and their location. Why candles? What do they evoke, and what symbolism do they recall?

How are they lit and extinguished? Who does this? When are they lit and when are they extinguished, and what does this say about worship in your space? Think again on the form (the thing itself), the content (What is the story? Why are they here?), and the meaning (how this connects with worship, with God, with the congregation).

These same questions of form-content-meaning would apply to the following elements:

Light fixtures

Flowers and plants

Projection screen

A cross

Organ pipes

Communion railings

How well do these fit together? Do the furnishings match? Is there a hodge-podge of wood colors and furniture styles? Does any of this add or detract to the worship experience? Are there ways to fashion more harmony and balance to what's on the platform? Is it enough to simply call attention to what's there in worship and preaching and to remind one another of the form, the function, and the meaning of what's there? Might these reminders also help a church decide what needs to remain and what might be placed elsewhere?

In a recent review of some of my photographs of the chancel areas of churches I'd visited, and in some cases served, I noticed how cluttered the chancel looked. In my direct experience with those sanctuaries I didn't find myself noticing the clutter, so why did I see it in the photographs? My answer, upon reflection, is that when we are present in a worship sanctuary we might in one moment presume an organic unity to all that is there, and in the next we focus on one object of attention. This focus keeps us from noticing the clutter, that which might be extraneous. One preaching strategy, then, could be to focus on the organic unity and then to focus on individual parts over time.

It would be interesting to bring in someone unfamiliar with worship spaces, hear the person's reactions to what is noticed, and draw lessons from the "unchurched" and whether one's space is inviting or off-putting.

It would be the preacher's choice how far to delve into these furnishings. Certainly references could be made along the way as a congregation begins to visually appreciate its worship sanctuary and learn to make connections with what is in the sanctuary with the worship of God and the nurture of the members' life together as a congregation.

Fabrics in Chancel and Nave

In this section I offer suggestions for other ways you can preach your worship space. A sermon or sermons could be devoted to highlighting the use of fabric in the worship space. Another set of messages could be devoted to the exterior of the church building and how its shape, color, and external features speak to what goes on in this place. Finally, you could also design a series of sermons on one or more of the artworks hanging throughout the church building.

Preaching the Fabrics

From time to time church members raise questions about the American flag and whether it is or is not to be displayed in the worship space. Many of us have served churches where the flags have been positioned in different locations over time, including not being in the sanctuary at all. With national attention often focused on flag etiquette, and who is or is not displaying flag symbols, these issues sometimes seep into church life.

At one church I served there was a question about the proper location of the U.S. flag and the Christian flag, whether they should be near the altar in the chancel or on the floor of the sanctuary, and on which sides, right or left?

Since we were approaching the July 4 holiday, it seemed like a good time to preach on the issue of flags in church, the history of their inclusion or exclusion in worship sanctuaries globally and in the United States, a variety of theological positions on the subject, and what this congregation's response might be.

It occurred to me I could also draw this out into a larger summer sermon series that included other fabrics in the worship space. Rather than focus solely on the issue of the flags – and possibly focus too much anxiety and heated feelings on the one topic – why not put that topic into the context of a larger series on what our fabrics say about whom we are as a church and what we are as God's people called to be servants of God's mission in the world?

This got me thinking about other fabrics in church:

Flags: Some churches include the U.S. flag as well as a Christian flag and perhaps a United Nations flag. Where these are located should reflect the U.S. Flag Code as set by Congress. If a choice is made to have them on display, then further choices include whether these are on the platform or the floor level. The U.S. flag is to be to the congregation's right side on the floor level. When the flag is on the platform or stage, however, the U.S. flag is to be to the speaker's right side and to the congregation's left.

Banners: What banners are hung, where, and when? Is there a liturgical focus to these banners, and what is the relationship of color, symbol, and words or phrases on these banners to our worship?

Drapes/draperies/curtains: Where might these be found in the sanctuary? Why are they there? Do the colors hold any significance? Is there any ceremonial or worship function to these fabrics? Is there a shading/lighting function they fulfill, or do they elicit a sense of mystery – what is behind the curtain, and should we know?

Altar cloths and paraments: Why do we place cloths on communion tables and altars? What is the significance of the colors and any symbols that are on these fabrics? What do these say about our worship and liturgy? What fabrics hang from the lectern and pulpit? These forms say something about our worship, and they have a context, or story, and then a number of meanings we can draw.

Vestments: What do the clergy wear while leading worship, and is this important? What are the variety of robes, albs, and chasubles that are worn? What is the history of these garments? What do the styles and colors have to say about the role and function of the clergy in our worship? What about stoles and their colors and symbols? What is their story, and what meanings do we draw from them? Are there trends away from wearing these formal vestments? If the clergy wear street clothes, is this appropriate, and what might this be telling us?

Dress codes: Does our church have a dress code for worship? Is the code clearly spelled out, or is it unspoken? What should we wear? Do we carry expectations? Standards? Anything goes? Does it matter, really? Is this essential or non-essential? Naming this subject is an important one and will elicit lots of response from church members, since it's a subject that's possibly addressed privately but seldom publicly. It would help to get these issues out on the table!

As part of my sermon series I developed a PowerPoint presentation that showed a number of people wearing different clothing, jewelry, and tattoos and invited the congregation's response as part of the sermon/message. I asked: Would this person be welcome in our church? Would this one? I also showed pictures of guide dogs and people in wheelchairs. The combined presentation on clothing and differing looks and abilities opened up the larger issue of who is really welcome to our worship.

In the next chapter I provide a model for preaching with your windows.

Chapter 3

Teaching Your Windows

The sanctuary windows are an important structural and decorative part of the church. Whether they are clear or stained glass, they deserve at least one if not a whole series of sermons.

There is a long and interesting history on the structural challenges involved in building massive church walls and including long sections of windows: One need look only to Notre Dame in Paris and the flying buttresses to see one solution to the problem of supporting heavy walls with holes in them: windows.

Other French churches such as St. Chapelle in Paris, St. Denis just outside of Paris, and the Cathedral at Chartres offer wonderful stories and experiences about the development of stained glass.

Sermons connecting this history with the history of one's own church building can be interesting, particularly as stories are told. Some of them are found in the windows themselves, with their stories, symbols, and colors, and how these are connected to church history and theology. Some stories are found in the names of persons or groups that gave windows as memorials and learning whom they were and what prompted the gifts.

For those churches without stained glass, there is also a history as to why they opted away from that, sometimes rooted in the iconoclastic movements of the Protestant Reformation and a commitment to simplicity, a suspicion of visual imagery, and a prejudice toward the preached/spoken word. Other times the presence of clear glass, particularly in more natural rural or suburban settings, serves to open the sanctuary to light and to the nature surrounding the church building.

Some windows are designed to be opened to bring in fresh air or to let out the sound of organ and singing. These functions also serve meanings that may be drawn out.

As you sit in the sanctuary you might notice how many windows there are on a wall: Does the number bear any significance? How many panes are in the windows? Does this number bear any significance? I have often noticed sets of six, seven, eight, and 12 in church windows, all non-verbally speaking to symbolisms we've already noticed in previous chapters.

As part of your studied observations with your sanctuary, you might notice how the light changes at different times of the day and how what the windows bring in changes with that light. How do different weather conditions affect the light – and mood – thrown by those windows? Is there a window with imagery in the front of the sanctuary, and what does that say to the gathered congregation? Is there a window with a story that all see as they enter or leave the narthex or the nave? What significance does that window and its story have for the worship congregation and worship itself?

For example, one church I served had a large stained glass picture of Jesus and a flock of sheep, and he was holding one sheep, presumably a reference to the parable of the lost sheep. This window was only seen as people left the worship sanctuary. When that church building was sold and a new one built, that window was moved to the new church. This time, the window was placed in the chancel area, where the window was seen throughout the entire worship service.

Rather than being a focus of leaving, representing how the congregation was sent out into the world to find comfort that Jesus seeks the lost, and that they too might follow him and do the same, the same imagery became a part of the worship experience. Did anything change? Was there a new emphasis that the worshipper might find comfort and belonging during worship but might not make a connection with how he or she is to also look for lost sheep in the world outside the sanctuary?

In other words, one placement of the window invited an outward response as the people left the church to return to the world, while the other placement of the window invited an inward response as people gathered for worship to be fed and found. Or not. The form is the stained glass window, the content is the story it tells, and the meaning, the "so what?" is in the eyes and heart of the interpreters, which means there is no one answer!

Preaching your windows involves spending time with each one. Many churches have individual stories represented in each window, shown as pictures, symbols, and colors. The pictures may depict references to biblical stories from the life of Jesus (lost sheep, knocking on a door, rescuing Peter from the water, at prayer), sacraments like baptism or communion, or even stories from the life of the congregation gathered in that church.

The pictures might be combined with symbols such as loaves of bread, sheaves of wheat, grapes, water, doves, flames, vines, light rays, or with historical Greek and Latin symbols such as the Alpha and Omega, the Chi Rho, or the INRI.

"If churches are made radiant and beautiful places of worship, we can have a spiritual regeneration without anyone knowing what is going on. Beauty can preach as very few men with bundles of words can preach. I want to make beautiful interiors for both churches and souls. I want men (*sic*) to hear my windows singing; to hear them singing of God. I want men (*sic*) to know that God is at the core of their own souls."

Charles J. Connick, whose studios made stained glass windows for churches for nearly 75 years

Stained glass windows contain a rich and colorful lexicon of biblical story and theological affirmation people have seen time and again and yet have never really noticed, much less understood the references. Preaching your windows invites the congregation into a new way of seeing their home sanctuary, and even visitors will get something out of this to take back to other sanctuaries they may visit.

Inviting people to look at the windows as you speak also offers an audiovisual presentation without needing any additional technology!

It has been my experience that people report they've worshipped in a sanctuary their entire lives and never noticed what was going on in those windows – and how people will always look at the windows differently from now on. That makes for a memorable sermon!

What follows is an example of how you could begin to reflect out loud in a sermon about the windows in your sanctuary. We can trust that my reference to south-side windows actually fits your sanctuary's orientation, but you can make your own adaptations.

What a wonderful testimony that you have put these memorial windows on the south side of the church. They face the side that receives the most morning light. How significant it is that they remind us of the light that God made in the beginning when all was dark and formless and the spirit of God hovered over it all and God said, "Let there be light!" There was light, that first light at the beginning, but more than that now, these windows bring in a light meant for us to enjoy on Sunday mornings. So, the windows also represent the first Easter morning and the light of resurrection faith.

The windows bring us the golden light of the fresh new morning, and they also bring us rich and vivid colors. You may not even be aware of this, because each contrasting color, as different and bold as it is, still serves the overall harmony and beauty that are ever gifts from God.

The great 20th century painter Wassily Kandinsky said that " . . . colour is a power which directly influences the soul. " He wrote a little book called *Concerning the Spiritual in Art.* (You might wish to buy his book and read directly from it as you preach your message.) He was fascinated with how colors reached into human souls with the complete and full power of the spiritual. He said colors produce a "spiritual vibration."

Look at the colors in the window, if you like, while I read to you how he describes some of the colors in the window and their spiritual flavor.

"Blue is the typical heavenly colour. The ultimate feeling it creates is one of rest." (Note, too, that we associate the color blue with water as well, and this color in your windows can refer to the waters of life, the waters of chaos out of which God brought life [see Gen. 1:1])

"Green is the most restful colour that exists . . . (I)t is the colour of summer, the period when nature is resting from the storms of winter and the productive energy of spring." (Green can refer to nature, life, growth, and even eternity.)

"Red . . . rings inwardly with a determined and powerful intensity." (Red, in the church, also refers to the Holy Spirit, or to renewal, in particular as found in the Pentecost story in Acts 2.)

The brown shows a "powerful inner harmony . . . an appeal of extraordinary, indescribable beauty." (It can also refer to the color of earth, of ground and soil, the foundation of life and agriculture.)

Yellow can refer to holiness, as God-light dispersed into human hearts or shaped as a halo over heads of Jesus, the disciples, angels, and other holy figures.

"Shades of colour," he wrote, "awake in the soul emotions too fine to be expressed in words."

Today we celebrate how we are surrounded by so great a cloud of witnesses who bring us testimony to the power of faith, hope, and love. These windows, indeed all the windows in this sanctuary, touch our souls with delicacy, beauty, and light. They speak of the relationship of a solid structure (the wall itself) and of a necessary openness (the windows). Together wall and window tell us something of the nature of the church: a vessel by which we bear witness to fragile grace, and to enlightening beauty.

Today we give thanks for those who have given us this beauty and who invite us, each time we gather in this sanctuary, to testify to God's abundant love for us.

These windows (in the case of memorial windows) could represent the losses of the past. The windows could remind us of the passing of a beloved minister; they could remind us of the loss of a beloved old church building; and of the losses of church members and servants of this church. But the beauty of these windows, the Easter faith to which they testify, best serves as a moving forward in confidence, a building of a healthy new congregation strong and vital, ready to greet the future with beauty, grace, and color.

If this is so, then it is time to turn the shadows of loss into the brightness of God's colorful and golden future. Let these windows stand for the faith, hope, and love of those who have gone on before us and who have dedicated their lives to this church. Let these windows be our comfort, our guide, and our inspiration as we rededicate ourselves to the uniqueness that is the (your church name here).

For as the writer of the Book of Hebrews (11:40-12:1) declares: " . . . since God had provided something better so that they (the dear ones we remember) would not, apart from us, be made perfect. Therefore, since we are surrounded by so great a cloud of witnesses, let us also lay aside every weight, and the sin which clings so closely, and let us run with perseverance the race that is set before us."

As we close these three chapters on the nave and chancel, we move into some additional preaching opportunities with architecture in the following chapter.

Note

The quotations in the discussion on colors are from Wassily Kandinsky, *Concerning the Spiritual in Art* (New York: Dover Publications, 1977), pp. 25 and 38.

Chapter 4

Additional Teaching Suggestions

In this chapter we'll look at a few other possibilities for preaching with illustrations from the rich visual library that is your church. The first example is based on the outside of your church building. The second example features a look at some of the artwork on display inside the church. We close with some thoughts on how all this can be pulled together into a series of sermons.

Teaching the Exterior

As part of your walk around the church, you might spend some time outside. Is the church site on a hill or a level surface? Is it a high point (elevation) in the community? Is the building raised up on steps? The theological significance of this, "going up" as the Psalmist writes in Psalms of Ascent as pilgrims walked up to Jerusalem, and symbolically going upward and heavenward as a spiritual pilgrimage, is often a nonverbal message found in a staircase or set of steps leading up to a church building. Is this theological commitment borne out in older architecture now an impediment to those who in today's world need more accessible facilities? Has the church accommodated these needs with ramps and/or elevators or an alternative entrance to help people access your space?

What is the shape of the exterior? How many exterior walls are there? How would you describe the general shape of the building? Does it follow a cross pattern? Does it look more like a ship or a boat?

How do the windows look from the outside? If they are stained glass, you don't see as much as you see from the inside. This in itself invites a meditation on stained glass windows and the "window" of our soul. People might look at those exterior windows and know they are windows but little else about them until people get inside and see the colors and stories. So, too, this might be how we appear: We see people on the outside but have little access to the full color and story of their lives, their inner worlds. These observations might round out the messages shaped around your windows as well (see previous chapter).

What else is there outside the building in the way of statues, installations, bell towers, crosses, artworks, plants, shrubs, and trees? How effective is your signage? Can people driving by see your sign and get information about your church they might be seeking? Do these connect with your church's message and mission? Are they inviting? What do they say about whom this congregation is and who is welcome?

What are the forms of your exterior, what is their story, how does that story connect to what goes on in your place, and what are some of the meanings of what is seen? Bringing this to the attention of the whole congregation in the context of the larger Christian story could make an interesting sermon series. Since your congregation is inside when the message is offered (unless you do offer this sermon during an outdoor worship where you are seated outside the building), you might wish to take pictures for the main preaching points and put them into a presentation program such as PowerPoint and project the photographs on a screen in the sanctuary so all can see what you've noticed from the church exterior.

Teaching With Your Church's Art

Most churches have popular religious paintings hanging on the walls. Some of these are stories from the Gospel accounts of the life of Jesus. Popular images include Sallman's "Head of Christ" (1941) and various versions of Leonardo da Vinci's "The Last Supper" (1495-98).

As with everything else in the church, many people walk by these pictures and give them little notice, while some people find comfort and meaning knowing the pictures are there.

One way to preach these pictures is to find an easel, and if they are large enough, bring them into the sanctuary so people can see them as you talk about their content and meaning. Alternatively you could find digital images of these same pictures on the Internet and project them on a projection screen so people can see a large image and even close-ups of details of the picture.

A sermon could include looking at the picture, identifying the particular biblical passage the picture illustrates, speak to what's known about the artist and the artist's commitment to the subject, and what meanings may be drawn for the life of the gathered congregation that day.

Since there are so many "Last Supper" pictures that refer to Leonardo's version, I have found that people enjoy seeing what other artists have done side by side and then comparing them with the original. This technique opens a lesson in interpretation and how artists preach their own vision of messages of the story in subtle and sometimes not so obvious ways. If nothing else, this teaches people how to look more closely at art and receive permission to study art and draw their own conclusions.

"A church living aesthetically will find itself breaking new ground. There will be a cessation of old, desiccated ways and, perchance, an ecstatic movement toward freedom."

John Westerhoff

I have preached this way and found people appreciate learning more about the art and artists that have been a part of people's churches for many years.

Another growing point for a congregation is to introduce it to other artists' depictions of these common biblical stories such as the Last Supper, the parable of the lost sheep, Christ knocking at the door, or the head of Christ. When done from a cross-cultural experience, and by bringing in the work of artists from Asia, Latin America, and Africa, a congregation's sense of global Christianity will grow. This will also show how a congregation's bias toward northern European art can limit the congregation's visual horizon.

The church I mentioned in the previous chapter that had the large stained glass image of Jesus with the lost sheep front and center for the congregation hadn't paid much attention to the fact that Jesus appears as a very white male. The other stained glass windows also showed Jesus as white European, as did the rest of the art around the church. Since the Sunday school was multiracial, it was essential to me to start bringing to the congregation the rich multicultural imagery of Jesus from around the world.

Using the blank white wall to the right of the pulpit as a projection screen, I developed regular PowerPoint presentations to show such things as the nativity of Christ from multicultural perspectives or some of the parables of Jesus. For our monthly communion Sundays we would show a variety of "last supper" images or of people eating together in different global settings. In a way this "wall" with the projected imagery became another stained glass window showing other stories from the life of Christ from varied sources.

On Doing A Sermon Series

Much of what we've discussed here can't be preached in just one sermon. The subject matter would take a series of sermons to effectively handle the vast amount of material touched upon in these pages. Besides being able to cover more about the architecture, furnishings, art, and fabrics of your church, a sermon series also seems to keep people attending.

Having a series is easy to promote, and a series such as this is unique and might well draw visitors. The preacher enjoys benefits from a series as well, as it's easy to structure and sets the way ahead for some weeks and even months. The series helps structure material and focus messages around a theme, heightening a sense of organization that sometimes is lost with the seeming randomness of lectionary preaching alone.

Summers are a good time for a sermon series of maybe 3-4 weeks. Sermon series are good in the summer because, if they are interesting enough to people, they will boost attendance. People might make an effort to attend all three or four weeks of your series.

That said, the fall is another good time for a sermon series when people are returning to church and when, if they are returning after a busy summer, they might respond well to fresh reminders of their identity as members of a particular congregation of the Body of Christ in their part of the world.

Certainly the topics I've discussed may be preached as stand-alone topics, but these topics could also be folded into other sermons, particularly when references may be made to something in the sanctuary that relates to your topic. For example, if you're preaching a Communion sermon, you could refer to the table itself and what it signifies, or you could refer to the words on the table, "This Do In Remembrance of Me," or to the Alpha and Omega that might also be carved into that table.

A sermon on a parable might also point to that same parable that happens to be illustrated in one of your windows. A Good Friday sermon could refer to the INRI found on a banner in the sanctuary or to the cross pattern (Greek or Latin) upon which the congregation gathers as it is seated in that nave.

Long ago theologian Paul Tillich reflected on how, over time, religious symbols can lose their meaning and become simply an unseen background.

As many churches struggle with their own relevance in a quickly changing world, describing the symbols, art, and architecture of one's worship space may just be enough to inspire congregations to move forward with new energy.

Chapter 5

Screens In Worship: "Framing" the Conversation

As worship communities move toward incorporating more visuals in worship, there are many questions about the projection screens that may be needed: how and when to use them, where to get them and in what size and material, whether it's even a good idea to use them at all, and even why not to use them!

While all of these questions are important ones to any congregation thinking about screens in worship, another conversation lurks behind it all: What is this thing called a "screen?" What does it have to do with God and the worship of God? Could it be the church has always used "screens" but we just haven't noticed?

Simply put, a projection screen is a framed surface upon which are projected colors, shapes, designs, pictures, and words.

The earliest surfaces used for expressing messages with color, shape, and picture were cave walls, where an available space was used by early artists to call attention to an essential event of daily life: the hunt. Early Christians used a similar surface, the walls of Roman-era catacombs, to portray essential events of daily life: eucharist and prayer.

The surfaces of these walls provided small spaces that were dedicated to the content – and the meaning – of human life. Some early wall art had no discernible frame, such as a free-formed picture of a bison, while later wall art, such as Michelangelo's Sistine Chapel ceiling, was framed by a combination of the architectural features of the ceiling and the lines of color the artist used to distinguish one panel of the frescoed mural from another.

Church interiors today employ a number of framed surfaces for communicating content and meaning: plain painted walls that sometimes include murals or pictures; colored-glass windows sometimes showing symbol, picture, and story; carved or painted wooden panels with story and symbol; stretched canvases painted with landscapes and human forms and framed as pictures; hanging fabrics with sewn or applied shapes, colors, symbols, and words.

Given this wide variety of framed panels already included in church interiors, the projection screen may be seen as another framed surface the church uses to display the content of religious faith through color, shape, pictures, and words.

A Surface for Storytelling

For millennia, people have understood the storytelling power of figures fashioned from light and shadow. Plato's "Allegory of the Cave," dating back 2,400 years, uses the analogy of a wall with shadows cast upon it by firelight to suggest a role of education is to help people understand the difference between what is real and what is a representation of reality. Philosophers and storytellers alike came to see the educational and artistic possibilities brought by a light source, a surface, and the casting of shadows.

Walls and other surfaces would become the means, through light and shadow, by which skilled performers would bring delight – and moral lessons – to audiences throughout the world. These artists tapped into the interplay of light and shadow and found ways to use shadows themselves as storytelling devices for fun and learning.

For at least 2,000 years magicians and acting troupes traveled through China, India, Indonesia, Asia Minor, and Europe sharing the craft of shadow puppetry, bringing their audiences imaginative worlds full of entertaining stories and morality tales. First using walls and later fabric screens, some of these performers understood the screen to be God's universe upon which they cast shadows of their hands and handmade puppets as characters in a divine drama.

The English word "screen" finds its origin in this relationship of light and shadow. Hundreds of years old, the first uses of the word referred to upright panels covered with leather, cloth, or heavy paper and set in front of the hearth to form a room divider and shield people from the direct heat of the fire. It's easy to imagine children sitting in the space between the fire and the screen, using their hands to make shadows on the screen and telling grand stories about these figures. These screens, like those of the shadow puppet theaters, became a place for playful imagination.

Techniques for intensifying and focusing lighting effects developed gradually over time. Early light projectors were constructed to shine light through painted glass and to show the pictures on room walls. One of the first light projectors was called a "magic lantern," and it was used to delight small audiences with picture stories shown on walls, sheets, and special fabric or paper screens. Images were painted on glass in various colors and projected on the wall of a small room.

In 1646 the Jesuit priest Athanasius Kircher wrote a paper called "The Great Art of Light and Darkness" and gave instructions for building one of these light projectors. While he loved to "astonish" his viewers with this new visual art, he also encouraged them to understand the images were not magically produced but occurred naturally through the relationship of a light source (a candle or sunlight), a mirror inside the projector, and the wall or screen upon which the colored pictures were shown. Eager to connect his projector and screen to his theology, Kircher is said to have actually traced rabbinical use of projected images back to Solomon's Temple in Jerusalem.

"People want screens because screens open the door to more stories, more images, more information, and more excitement than ever before."

Kevin Roberts

As photography and motion picture technologies advanced in the 19th and early 20th centuries, churches began to use technically impressive projectors and screens to raise awareness and develop support for important mission projects. In 1908 the Foreign Christian Missions Society used a screen and projector in the Central Christian Church of Indianapolis to show church delegates stereopticon slides and picture films of missionary work in Japan, China, India, and Africa.

With the continued advancement of early motion picture technology, a number of clergy and laity in the United States advocated using movies and screens in worship services. Thomas Edison gave his blessing to these projects with an article he wrote for a church periodical in 1910.

During the course of the 20th century churches began to use other types of projection equipment in education and worship, including filmstrip projectors, 35mm slide projectors, opaque projectors, and transparency projectors, and projected picture and color onto walls and screens developed for that purpose.

A Window to the Holy Imagination

A screen, then, can be any surface upon which or through which light, shadow, and color may be projected. The screen itself may be a wall, a piece of colored or translucent fabric stretched on a wooden frame or attached to adjacent walls by taut lines, an unrolled synthetic white or gray surface stood on a tripod, or a specialized material suitable for video/data projectors raised and lowered from a narrow case by means of electric motor. The screen may consist of a reflective material upon which light is cast, similar to a typical filmstrip or slide-projector screen, or a translucent material such as thin fabric or a synthetic material best suited for video/data projectors. With translucent material, the light projector may be in front of or behind the screen.

The screen becomes a window for seeing the world, as the whole world can be shown on and through this window. It becomes a panel for displaying God's universe through the relationship of light and word, as at the beginning of creation when God said, "Let there be light." The screen becomes an artistic canvas for church artists to develop their holy imagination to show the worshipping community the relationship of God, Jesus Christ, and the Holy Spirit with all of creation.

Framing it in this way, we might begin to see a screen as just another framed surface on a church wall.

Think of the screen as the wall, the page, the panels, the window, the mosaic, the painting, the fresco, or the fabric art. The screen becomes any of the framed surfaces the church has used to show its story with pictures, symbols, and words:

A catacomb wall
A printed page of words
An illuminated manuscript with word and picture
A painted wood altarpiece
A stained glass window
A mosaic
A stretched and painted canvas
A frescoed wall panel
Fabric art
A framed photograph
A movie screen
A flat screen television

A screen can show clear and large any of these classical art forms:

A picture of praying figures from the catacombs
A page from any Bible or illuminated manuscript
The panels of a medieval wood altarpiece
A stained glass window from any church
A mosaic from the apse of a basilica
An oil painting of a bible story
A frescoed wall panel from the time of Renaissance
A piece of fabric art
Photography of important subjects

Looking at screens in this way, that what is shown on them fits the worship, educational, and mission life of the church, and a church can display a different content on its screens than that experienced by most people on the screens they experience at home, at work, and at school.

The apostle Paul wrote about the relationship of light, darkness, and the Christian community in his letter to the church at Corinth: "For it is the God who said, 'Let light shine out of darkness,' who has shone in our hearts to give the light of the knowledge of the glory of God in the face of Jesus Christ." (2 Cor. 4:6)

Light projected through and upon worship screens helps the community grow in its understanding of the content and meaning of Christian faith. The screen can become a means for the church to be in relationship with people who are eager to learn more and to grow in faith. Through engagement with the world and the positive influence of the creative arts to sensitize and grow awareness, people hear and respond to a calling to ministry in fresh, new and ever imaginative ways.

In the next chapter we'll look at common questions raised by clergy who just aren't convinced of the value of introducing screens and visual arts into worship in this second decade of the 21st century.

Chapter 6

Exercises

In this chapter we will look at pictures from several worship sanctuaries and put to practice some of the principles described in the chapters in Part III. Using a form-content-meaning method, I will draw out information from each photograph, and invite you to do the same. We'll end each example with some possible preaching directions for each picture.

A Method for Interacting With A Worship Space

Form: what we see: structural features, furnishings, fabrics, symbols.

Content: The stories told and references made: to biblical stories, to theological symbols, to a congregation's history, to a particular worship event.

Meaning: Possible interpretations and lessons drawn from the forms and content.

Preaching possibilities: Suggestions for drawing a congregation's attention to the forms, stories, and meanings of a worship space.

Form: The photograph is of stained glass windows on the west wall of St. John's United Church of Christ in Hartford, Wisconsin. There are eight sections of windows framed with wood. There are four long windows, two four-sided kite-like framed shapes at the top of each pair of long windows, and topping it all off is a circle with twelve panes, beneath which is a small triangle. Each of the four long windows has eight sections starting with a bottom rectangular section, above which are six smaller rectangles. The other panels include oval shapes, with a symbol in the fourth section of panels in each of the four long vertical sets of windows.

Content: Historical records show this sanctuary was built in 1907, and we might assume the windows were installed at that time. Colors include pale white, brown, green, and pink. In the fourth panel counting from the bottom is a representation of a *fleur-de-lis*, a lily. There is a bright light on the upper left side of these windows coming from sunshine through similar windows directly across on the east wall.

Meaning: Numbers: The round circle at the top could represent the world or a circle of eternity or a clock face with twelve panels – twelve hours? twelve months in a year? twelve tribes? twelve disciples? The four-sided diamond shapes could be three triangles divided in half (Trinitarian symbolism), and each includes eight panels (six represents creation of heaven and earth, seven represents rest and worship, eight might represent a transcending beyond the physical and spiritual and a fresh beginning). Overall, there are eight large sections framed by the wood, and each pair of windows has eight ovals in each horizontal section. The rectangular base could be the foundation, and the six smaller rectangular brick-like panels could be the structure of earth/life resting upon the seventh day as the day of rest and worship.

The three petals of the lily may represent the Holy Trinity, with the horizontal band at the middle symbolizing Mary, the mother of Jesus. The flower might also symbolize both the Annunciation to Mary and the Resurrection of Christ, and the ovals tucked beneath the drooping flower stalks might represent joy, renewal, or unconditional love. The earthy browns and vivid greens might recall soil and plants, the natural world of a religious community gathered to worship.

St. John's United Church of Christ, Hartford, Wisconsin

Preaching possibilities: Draw out meanings of light coming into the sanctuary; the number symbolisms of six, seven, and eight and what that means for a worship community; the passage of time with the clock-like window at the top, the fresh beginning of a week opening with worship; the meanings of the lily with its many references to biblical stories. These windows do more than bring a glorious light into the worship sanctuary: they feed imaginations and open hearts and minds to spiritual beauty.

Form: The photograph is of the chancel area of Union-Congregational UCC in Waupun, Wisconsin. Three steps lead to the chancel with a choir at the upper left, with a window with six panels, a draped cross on the back wall, a communion table or altar with a book on the table and a candle in front of the table, resting upon fabric reading "Holy Holy Holy." Front left is a smaller lectern, and to the right is a larger pulpit, each with fabric and a symbol of a crown. Behind the pulpit is a projection screen with fabric extending below. An unseen projector is behind the screen. On the floor level (the nave) are three rows of armed chairs in the front and behind are pews.

Content: A color image would show purple cloths, so the church is presumably decorated for Advent or Lent. The simplicity of the space without further decoration might suggest Lent, as would the draping of the cross. Three steps up might recall the Holy Trinity; the "Holy Holy Holy" reference is to Isaiah 6:3 or to the hymn of the same name. The crown could be a reference to the crown of thorns put on Jesus' head by Roman soldiers in John 19:2 or to the hymn "Crown Him With Many Crowns." The screen is anchored to the right wall and is behind the pulpit. The screen is ready to show words, pictures, or both and bring more content into the room. There is an invisible line from cross to the pulpit and from cross to the lectern, showing a relationship between the three.

Meaning: What do the colors, symbols, and words of Lent mean for a gathered congregation? What does it mean that the screen is located where it is? How do the furnishings covered with fabric connect with one another, and what might that mean for the worship life of a congregation gathered in that space?

Preaching possibilities: One sermon could focus on the fabrics and their connection (color, words, symbols, biblical references) to the Lenten story. Another sermon could focus on the chancel area as a place set apart from the nave and what function that serves in worship and the life of the church. For example, one could reflect on the function of the people who lead worship from the chancel (pastor, choir, liturgists, etc.). Yet another could focus on the purpose and function of the relationship of cross, altar/table, lectern, and pulpit. One could talk about the location of the screen and why it is

Union-Congregational UCC, Waupun, Wisconsin

located behind the pulpit. While a wall serves as a convenient anchor, the screen is also positioned behind the place in the chancel where the word is preached: the pulpit. Since we "read" from left to right, the preacher might best stand at the lectern or in the middle of the chancel when imagery is posted on the screen. Noting the distance between lectern, where scripture is read, and the pulpit, where the word is preached, one can talk about the interpretive tension between the two.

Form: The photograph is of the sanctuary of Ozark Prairie Presbyterian Church in Mt. Vernon, Missouri. Looking at the front from left to right we see:

An organ, a woman behind a small lectern with a white cloth on it, a U.S. flag, a man standing at a pulpit with white cloth on it, three chairs with cross-like structures, a large picture of a bearded man in a white robe draped with a colored cloth and arms outstretched, a slightly crooked projected image, below the image is a candleabra with seven candles, in front of this is a table or altar with a floral arrangement; visible beneath are three steps below, and off to the right is a cross topped with a thorny crown and draped with a white cloth, with a church flag to the right. Below the cross is a small projector on a stack of books, and just visible to the right of that is a computer screen. Looking up we see three light fixtures, and a ceiling line evoking a triangle.

Content: This is during a denominational business meeting. The central picture is Jesus in a welcoming pose. The projected image uses a light-colored wall for adequate contrast and visibility. The U.S. flag is properly situated at the speaker's right on the platform. The white cloths are seasonal in a church, usually used at Christmas and Easter, and with the draped cross and crown of thorns we could presume the Easter season.

Meaning: The chancel is three steps up, showing a Trinitarian symbolism, and there are three chairs as well. The tallest chair might be for the honored speaker or preacher. The cross represents the crucifixion of Jesus, and the thorny crown shows suffering even as the white cloth (the burial shroud?) evokes resurrection and John 20:6. What does it mean that of the two flags present, the U.S. flag and the Christian flag, that the U.S. flag is very close to the pulpit? Is this for a reason?

Preaching possibilities: One sermon could focus on the Easter themes with the white cloths. Another could focus on questions raised and statements made by the positioning of the flags. Another message could focus on the nature of Calvinistic Presbyterianism and its iconoclastic history and suspicion of imagery in worship in relation to all the imagery in the chancel. What is the history of the Jesus picture in that sanctuary and how does it match up with or conflict with an anti-imagery tradition? Does this invite using projected images in worship where once this would never be considered?

Ozark Prairie Presbyterian Church, Mt. Vernon, Missouri

Form: This photograph shows the nave and chancel area of the former University Christian Church in Berkeley, California. The church provides a very unique example of the imaginative use of fabric in a sanctuary. What is shown is a temporary fabric installation that implies lightness and delicacy while capturing visual attention.

Content: The church is hosting a special lecture event sponsored by the Pacific School of Religion in 2010, "Spiritual But Not Religious: Chasing the Divine." We see a ceiling with wooden rafters, below which hangs a translucent fabric as a kind of canopy inside the worship space. The separate arms of the fabric soar upward. At the left edge the fabric is shaped as a screen for a projected image. There is a single stained glass window at the front wall with what looks to be a cross shape. In front of that is another temporary installation that involves colored panels.

Meaning: Do the wooden rafters seem like an ark-like structure or more barn-like? What feelings does the natural wood evoke? Do the rafters provide structural stability and more of a visual backdrop to the space than anything symbolic? There is a thematic connection with the hand imagery on the central colored panels repeated with the image on the fabric screen. The hand has a hole in it, like a sun with beams of light. There is a sense of both immanence and transcendence in the hand: practical "hands-on" work in the world, joined with meditation and prayer. Note how the white fabric serves as a kind of canopy that captures attention while also functioning as a screen inviting an imaginative aesthetic.

Preaching possibilities: What do the fabrics evoke as they soar upward? How does the interaction of permanent structure, temporary installation, color, fabric, symbol, and light draw out the theme of "Chasing the Divine"? With so much going on visually, how does the spoken word interact with the visual "word" as presented? A preacher could engage the congregation by asking questions about its experience with the space. What does it look like from the congregation's perspective? What does the space feel like? How does it fit the theme?

University Christian Church, Berkeley, California

Form: This photograph shows the Cocoa Beach Community Church in Cocoa Beach, Florida, immediately following a Sunday worship service.

Content: There is a ceiling with wooden rafters. At the front are three stained glass windows and two flat screen televisions to either side. Light fixtures seem to be in groups of three. There is a U.S. flag off to the left on the platform, but the flag is not prominently displayed. To the right of it is an organ, with a baptismal font on the floor in front of the organ, and in the center is an altar or communion table. The pulpit is on the far right side behind a wooden box.

Meaning: Do the wooden rafters seem more barn-like, remembering the birth of Jesus in a stable? What feelings does the natural wood evoke? There are triangular shapes in the ceiling, as well as three steps leading up to the chancel, invoking Trinitarian symbolism. There is a visual balance in the chancel with the three stained glass windows flanked by the two flat screens. The angle of the walls seems to indicate an octagonal shape, with three walls in the front, long side walls to the back, and three angled walls at the rear. The eight sides, as noted before, might remind the community of how worship in this space calls forth fresh beginnings in a new day.

Preaching possibilities: The three windows and two screens provide a group of five referring to the first five books of the Pentateuch or Torah, used for instruction. The three-panel central stained glass window and the two on the side, while not clear to us in this picture, yet have stories to tell that could be preached. During worship the flat screens were used to show hymns to songs and prayers and to post announcements after the service was finished. The screens were turned off during the sermon. They could be used to add additional imagery to a sermon. For example, during a sermon on the stained glass windows, close-up images of certain features of the windows could be displayed on the screens for people to get a better view. Given the three windows, the lights in groups of three, and the rafters in triangles, a sermon on the meaning of such Trinitarian symbolism for that particular congregation might prove interesting to them.

Cocoa Beach Community Church, Cocoa Beach, Florida

Form: This photograph is taken of St. John's United Church of Christ in Hartford, Wisconsin. At the front on the floor level is a table with a white cloth. Two steps up is the platform, where on the right is a lectern with an open book and a symbol or pattern of three overlapping ovals and on the left is a partial view of a pulpit with a similar cloth. A baptismal font is directly in front of the pulpit. An organ is behind the pulpit and a bench behind the lectern. Up three more steps is the chancel, marked by the wooden railings on either side, and at the top is an altar with a cloth, a Bible, a floral arrangement, and two candles. Centered behind is a Latin cross. The wooden screen behind the altar is, like the windows from the same church, using groups of four panels. To the top above the cross there are five niches and a small carved cross on either side. Below each of the small crosses is a line of seven small squares. Two banners flank this screen, each with a picture of a candle, and one with the word "Jesus" and the other with the word "joy."

Content: The table on the floor level is a communion table, signaled by the words, partially obscured by bright sunshine flooding the table, "This Do In Remembrance of Me" from I Corinthians 11:24. This would make the furnishing directly beneath the central cross an altar. The communion table would hold the communion elements, while the altar would be the place to present offerings.

Meaning: There are a cross below the communion table and two shrine-like openings on either side. The cross has the symbol IHS on it, Greek letters for the words Jesus, Son, Savior. The symbol on the visible altar cloths looks like a summary of the *IXTHUS*, a Greek anagram for "Jesus Christ, God's Son, Savior." When the letters are drawn together in a circle, two patterns may be seen: a Greek cross and what looks to the modern eye to be an airplane propeller. The "propeller" image on the altar cloth may represent this shape. As it is now it may evoke the Trinity. The flames of the altar candles might represent the light of God's presence during worship, and the flames on the banners might represent Jesus as light of the world (John 8:12). On the large wooden piece behind the altar the sets of four panels add to eight across and follow the "eighth day" motif as a fresh beginning. The seven small squares might represent the six days of creation and the seventh day of rest and worship, and the five niches at the top might represent the first five books of Moses in the Old Testament. Three niches on the front of the altar speak of

St. John's United Church of Christ, Hartford, Wisconsin

Trinitarian symbolism. Pews visible in the chancel are to be used by the choir.

Preaching possibilities: A sermon could discuss the difference between a communion table and an altar. The separate chancel invites discussion of what is held most sacred at the altar area: cross, Bible, Trinity, an altar for offerings, and a place for the choir. Why are these given a favored position, and what does that mean biblically and theologically?

Form: This is a photograph of one stained glass window in a set of eight at St. John's United Church of Christ in Slinger, Wisconsin. The windows were dedicated in 1950 in the original church building and later moved to the new facility.

Content: A picture is set in an oval shape. Along the sides of the whole window are what seem to be curling branches with leaves, and above and below the oval are flowers and leaves. Two curling arrows may be seen on either side of the oval, pointing towards the oval. The picture in the oval is of a star with three different kinds of light beams, one set circling the star itself, another pointing outward, and the third set flowing downward to a small covered area. The star seems to be beneath a dome with curling smoke or clouds just above the roof. Light rays seem to point to a flower on a bed of hay resting in a feeding trough or manger, below which is the stem of the plant with hay or ground on either side.

Meaning: The picture speaks to the birth of Jesus at Bethlehem (Luke 2:7) where the child is laid in a manger. A star shines overhead (Matthew 2:2). The rose may be from Song of Solomon 2:1, "I am the rose of Sharon . . . " sometimes applied to Jesus as perfect and beautiful and as one who loves. The leaves below the manger and below the oval seem more like those of the acanthus plant, a symbol of immortality.

Preaching possibilities: Using this window in a Christmas sermon could draw out the symbols associated with the birth of Jesus: star, manger, rose, acanthus leaves. There is also a cross pattern on the vertical from star to plant and the horizontal of the roof. Birth, death, and resurrection are found in this window, recalling lines from the third verse of Charles Wesley's hymn "Hark! the Herald Angels Sing:" "Hail the heaven born Prince of Peace! Hail the Son of righteousness, Light and life to all he brings, risen with healing in his wings."

St. John's United Church of Christ, Slinger, Wisconsin

I extend my thanks to the following churches for inviting me into their spaces, for what I have learned from them, and for the photographed images included in this book:

Cocoa Beach Community Church UCC, Cocoa Beach, Florida
Epworth United Methodist Church, Berkeley, California
Ozark Prairie Presbyterian "Brick" Church, Mt. Vernon, Missouri
St. John's United Church of Christ, Hartford, Wisconsin
St. John's United Church of Christ, Slinger, Wisconsin
St. Luke's United Methodist Church, Dubuque, Iowa
Union-Congregational Church UCC, Waupun, Wisconsin
University Christian Church, Berkeley, California.

About the Highlighted Quotations

Chapter 2 – Kent C. Bloomer and Charles W. Moore, *Body, Memory, and Architecture* (New Haven: Yale University Press, 1977).

Chapter 3 – Charles J. Connick, whose studios made stained glass windows for churches for nearly 75 years in the 20th century.

Chapter 4 – John H. Westerhoff III, *Will Our Children Have Faith?* (Harrisburg, Pennsylvania: Morehouse Publishing, 2000).

Chapter 5 – Kevin Roberts (kevinjroberts.net)

About the Author

The Rev. Michael Bausch, D. Min., is an ordained minister, author, and educator who teaches the use of the arts and multimedia in worship based on many years of parish ministry experience in the United Church of Christ. Over the years he has been a keynote speaker at a large number of UCC and Presbyterian denominational events.

His teaching experience includes offering summer courses in the subject for several years at the Graduate Theological Union in Berkeley and in a number of other mainline seminaries, including the University of Dubuque Theological Seminary, the Vancouver School of Theology, United Theological Seminary of the Twin Cities, and Luther Seminary. Besides teaching biblical studies courses at the University of Wisconsin-Platteville, he has extensive online teaching experience that includes developing and teaching courses at undergraduate and graduate levels, including summer online courses for the Pacific School of Religion.

His books include *A Media Sourcebook* (Pacific School of Religion, 1973), *Everflowing Streams: Songs for Worship* (with Ruth Duck, The Pilgrim Press, 1981), and *Silver Screen, Sacred Story: Using Multimedia in Worship* (The Alban Institute, 2002). He has written numerous articles for publications such as *The Clergy Journal*, *Liturgy: Journal of the Liturgical Conference,* and *Church Educator.*

More recent books include:

Feeding Imaginations: Worship That Engages (2015)
Drawn In: Dramatic Encounters With Art (2017)
Saturday Morning and Other Stories (2022)

Presently he is serving as an Annuitant Visitor for the Pension Boards, United Church of Christ, in the Southwest Wisconsin Association. Other interests include playing guitar and harmonica with several musical groups, and playing tennis and pickleball.

www.ingramcontent.com/pod-product-compliance
Lightning Source LLC
LaVergne TN
LVHW050344160826
845677LV00014B/3778

* 9 7 9 8 3 6 7 9 5 2 0 0 1 *